What Was World War I?

by Nico Medina

illustrated by Dede Putra

Penguin Workshop

For Uncle Bill "Sir Yes Sir!" Salter
& the War Department—NM

PENGUIN WORKSHOP
An imprint of Penguin Random House LLC, New York

First published in the United States of America by Penguin Workshop,
an imprint of Penguin Random House LLC, New York, 2023

Visit us online at penguinrandomhouse.com.

Library of Congress Cataloging-in-Publication Data is available.

Printed in the United States of America

ISBN 9780593521656 (paperback)   10 9 8 7 6 5 4 3 2 1 WOR
ISBN 9780593521663 (library binding)   10 9 8 7 6 5 4 3 2 1 WOR

Contents

What Was World War I?

By late December 1914, a war in Europe had been raging for more than four months. The armies fighting against one another were holed up inside deep trenches.

Twin lines of these trenches zigzagged five hundred miles from Switzerland all the way to the North Sea. This was the Western Front in the bloody war. (Fighting was also taking place in eastern Europe.) Defending one line of trenches were soldiers from Great Britain, Belgium, and France. Behind the other line was the German army.

Western Front, 1914–1918

No-man's-land on the Western Front

In between the trenches was a wide expanse known as no-man's-land. It was about 250 yards across and laden with barbed wire. Littered with abandoned military equipment and fallen soldiers, no-man's-land was extremely dangerous to cross.

The trenches were three to six feet wide and up to ten feet deep. They were disgusting places, muddy and full of rodents. But they offered troops some protection from enemy fire—if they kept their heads down! New kinds of rifles were being used and could fire from longer distances than ever before. And heavy artillery shells from each side blasted deep holes in the ground and could blow soldiers' bodies apart.

Battles along the trench lines dragged on for weeks or months, not days. Attack after attack was repelled by the other side. Often there was no clear victory. Neither army gained much ground, and the bodies kept piling up. In just one day at the Battle of the Somme, more than nineteen thousand British soldiers died.

It was a vicious kind of warfare never seen before. But for one day that winter, there was a moment of peace and goodwill.

On Christmas Eve, British soldiers in Belgium heard something coming from the other side of no-man's-land. The Germans were singing Christmas carols! The British soldiers began singing, too.

"Come over here!" one German soldier shouted in English.

"You come halfway, I come halfway!" replied one of the British sergeants.

And so they did!

The two groups of soldiers climbed cautiously out of their trenches and stepped into no-man's-land. They met in the middle and shook hands, wishing one another a Merry Christmas.

Gifts of cigarettes, wine, and sweets were exchanged. Christmas trees were lit with candles.

The celebration lasted all night and into Christmas Day, when a friendly game of soccer took place.

"How marvelously wonderful, yet how strange it was," a German lieutenant later wrote. "Christmas, the celebration of love, managed to bring mortal enemies together as friends for a time."

The Christmas Truce was celebrated by as many as one hundred thousand soldiers, all along the Western Front. But it didn't last long. The following day, both sides went right back to killing each other.

Many of these men and boys had expected to be home for the holidays. Their countries' leaders had said the war would be over quickly. But it would be almost four more years before it ended.

In World War I, Germany and its allies, the Central Powers, battled the Allied forces of France, Great Britain, and Russia (and eventually the United States) across four continents—on land, in the air, and at sea. Advances in weaponry—tanks, machine guns, poison gas, warplanes—led to unimaginable death tolls and near-total destruction.

More than nine million soldiers were killed, and more than twenty-one million wounded. Millions more were imprisoned or went missing. As many as thirteen million civilians died of starvation, disease, or at the hands of invading forces.

By the time Germany lost the war, its population was starving and its economy lay in ruins. Its empire had crumbled, along with the royal monarchies of Austria-Hungary and Russia. Europe and the world were forever changed.

How had this all come to pass?

A War with Many Names

Before 1914, wars had usually been local, between two combatant powers. Now there was a global struggle fought on several continents. At first, it was known as the Great War. It was also called the Kaiser's War, or Kaiser Bill's War. (*Kaiser* means "emperor," and "Bill" was Wilhelm II, Germany's leader.) Some called it the War to End All Wars, which sadly it wasn't. It became known as World War I once World War II began in Europe in 1939.

CHAPTER 1
Rival Empires

In 1914, the world looked very different than it does today. Africa and South Asia were largely ruled by the British and French empires. Raw materials from France's and Britain's overseas colonies made the empires very rich and powerful.

Germany was still a young nation. Once a collection of small kingdoms, it had unified only in 1871. But Germany modernized rapidly.

Germany's leader, Kaiser Wilhelm II, believed the only way for his country to remain secure was to become the world's most powerful empire. So Germany began to build factories, ports, and railways. It also expanded its military, stockpiled weapons, and took over parts of Africa, Asia, and several Pacific islands.

German soldiers

France and Germany were neighbors—and bitter rivals. They had fought many wars over the years and did not trust each other. France and Great Britain watched Germany's rise with alarm. So did Russia, Germany's neighbor to the east.

What if Germany tried to expand its empire within Europe?

Wilhelm II (1859–1941)

Kaiser Wilhelm II ruled Germany from 1888 until 1918. Wilhelm was born with a withered left arm—six inches shorter than his right. He had a fiery temper and a fondness for wearing military uniforms. Germany was a military dictatorship—Wilhelm and his generals believed in the strength of the armed forces above all else. He did not answer to his people. The day before World War I ended in 1918, the kaiser fled to the neighboring Netherlands, where he lived until his death.

France, Russia, and Great Britain decided to form alliances with one another. (An alliance is like a partnership between countries.) Alliances meant security and protection. If one country in an alliance was attacked, its allies would defend it.

Germany, surrounded by enemies, formed an alliance with its other neighbor, Austria-Hungary. The Austro-Hungarian Empire covered much of Central Europe. Franz Joseph I was its ruler.

Franz Joseph I (1830–1916)

Franz Joseph I's family, the Hapsburgs, had ruled Austria since the 1200s. In 1867, Franz Joseph made a deal with Hungary, a powerful kingdom ruled by Austria at the time. Austria and Hungary became equal partners in a "dual monarchy"—the Austro-Hungarian Empire—and Franz Joseph I became its leader.

Franz Joseph's personal life was filled with tragedy. His wife was assassinated, his son took his own life, and his brother, the emperor of Mexico, was executed by firing squad.

Franz Joseph led his empire into World War I in 1914. Unlike many of his family members, he lived a long life but did not live to see the end of the war.

Some fifty million people lived in the Austro-Hungarian Empire. They came from many cultures and spoke more than a dozen languages. They didn't feel like part of one empire. Each different area felt separate. Franz Joseph worried that some might try to form their own nations.

In 1908, Franz Joseph took over a small nation called Bosnia. Bosnia's neighbor was Serbia, which had become independent in 1878. (Both countries had formerly been part of another vast empire, the Ottoman Empire.)

Many Serbians encouraged Bosnia—and other places under Austro-Hungarian rule—to become a part of *their* new country.

Did Franz Joseph like this? Absolutely not. He did not want to give up any of his empire.

Perhaps a quick, decisive war against Serbia would make other countries think twice before challenging the Austro-Hungarian Empire.

What would be the spark to ignite such a war?

CHAPTER 2
One Wrong Turn in Sarajevo

Archduke Franz Ferdinand

On June 28, 1914, a nephew of Franz Joseph's visited the city of Sarajevo, the capital of Bosnia. He was fifty years old and an important nobleman: Archduke Franz Ferdinand. Someday, after his uncle died, Franz Ferdinand would become the emperor of Austria-Hungary—and rule over Bosnia.

The people of Bosnia felt insulted by the archduke's visit. It had to do with the date he chose to come. It was a solemn day in their history—five centuries before, the region had been conquered by the Ottoman Empire. Angry at this show of disrespect, a group of young men armed themselves with guns and explosives.

Unwisely, the archduke ignored warnings about plots against his life. He and his wife, Sophie, even rode in the back of their convertible with the top down! His motorcade's planned route had been published in newspapers ahead of his visit. So the terrorists knew exactly where to wait for him.

As the motorcade proceeded through Sarajevo, a bomb was thrown at the archduke's car. It bounced off the rear and exploded underneath the car behind the royal couple, injuring several people, including an official in the car. But the archduke and his wife were unharmed.

Franz Ferdinand refused to cancel the rest of his trip. He met with the mayor, as planned. Afterward, the archduke decided to visit the hospital to see the official who had been wounded by the bomb. For safety reasons, it was decided the archduke would take a different route out of the city. But his driver didn't speak German and did not understand the new plan!

One fateful turn brought the archduke and his wife directly to the street where nineteen-year-old Gavrilo Princip was waiting.

Gavrilo Princip

A Bosnian official riding with the royal couple told the driver he had gone the wrong way. The driver tried to reverse, but the car stalled.

Princip stepped onto the running board of the convertible and fired two shots, hitting the archduke in the neck and Sophie in the stomach.

An hour later, Franz Ferdinand and his wife were dead.

Princip and the other terrorists were Serbian. They had been armed and trained in their country then snuck across the border into Bosnia. Because of this, Austria-Hungary blamed Serbia for the archduke's murder.

Now Franz Joseph felt it necessary to start a war. He intended to make Serbia part of his empire. This would discourage the nations within the Austro-Hungarian Empire from declaring their independence.

But Franz Joseph worried Serbia's good friend Russia might come to its defense. So he approached his friend Kaiser Wilhelm II. The kaiser pledged Germany's full support for Franz Joseph if war broke out. Like Franz Joseph, the kaiser saw the war as an opportunity to crush his rivals and expand his empire.

On July 28, 1914, Austria-Hungary declared

war on Serbia. After that, it was like a row of dominoes falling. Soon, nearly all of Europe had taken sides: the Allies (France, Great Britain, and Russia) versus the Central Powers of Germany and Austria-Hungary.

One wrong turn and a fatal gunshot were all it took to spark what would become a worldwide war.

Warring Cousins

Victoria, Queen of England from 1837 to 1901, had nine children who married into royal families across Europe. One of her nicknames is the "grandmother of Europe."

Victoria's oldest daughter, Princess Royal Victoria (called Vicky), married a German emperor. Their son became Kaiser Wilhelm II. The queen's grandson George inherited the British throne in 1910 after the death of his father.

King George V

Queen Victoria's granddaughter Alexandra married Tsar Nicholas II of Russia. *Tsar* (say: ZAR) means "emperor."

Tsar Nicholas II

So three of the warring European leaders—King George V, Tsar Nicholas II, and Kaiser Wilhelm II—were all cousins or cousins-in-law! Wilhelm once said that if their grandmother had been alive in 1914, she would never have allowed the war to begin.

CHAPTER 3
A Different Kind of War

World War I was different from previous wars. Before, armies relied on horses to transport equipment and charge into battle. But now, the steam engine and railroads—and later,

the automobile—made it easier to move soldiers and supplies from place to place. Technology advanced rapidly during World War I. Horses were still used during the war, but by the end, soldiers on horseback had largely become a thing of the past.

The sheer size of the armies was historic. More than sixty-five million men served, nearly the entire population of Great Britain today!

When war broke out, there were fewer than half a million soldiers in the British army. Barely one month later, the British army had doubled in size. Becoming a soldier was a way to show pride in your country.

While men had to be eighteen to enlist, as many as 250,000 British boys—some as young

A young soldier

as fourteen—lied about their age to join the army. Many of these boys were poor, with few opportunities at home. Others were simply seeking adventure. Most were rejected if the lie was discovered. But as adult volunteers dwindled, officers were desperate to recruit troops. Some pretended not to know how young these brand-new soldiers were.

France and Great Britain also relied on troops from their overseas colonies. Hundreds of thousands of volunteers joined the British army—from the Caribbean to Canada, to India and Australia. France drafted men in its colonies into military service. The men had no choice. Still, many volunteered.

To arm these million-man armies, factories churned out military equipment and weapons that were deadlier than ever . . .

Flamethrowers shooting burning-hot oil across great distances.

Machine guns firing up to six hundred rounds per minute.

Long-range artillery weapons, like Germany's "Big Bertha," which could fire two-thousand-pound shells up to nine miles. Big Bertha required 240 men to assemble, operate, and

An Indian soldier

maintain it. It was so heavy—forty-seven tons—it had to be pulled by thirty-six horses.

Weapons like Big Bertha changed the way war was fought. Before, battles took place at much closer range, face-to-face. Only the front lines of soldiers could be attacked. Now, shells could be fired farther, exploding on impact at an army's front *and* rear flanks.

Big Bertha

The flood of men and new weapons meant that World War I's battles lasted longer and were deadlier than any that came before. Two of the

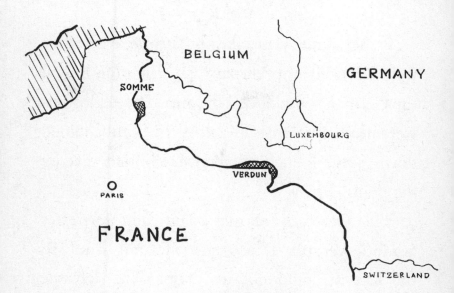

war's bloodiest and longest battles took place in France in 1916, at Verdun and the Somme River.

German general Erich von Falkenhayn wanted the Battle of Verdun to "bleed France white." His forces spent weeks building supply lines toward the French fortress city near the German border. Two and a half million shells were delivered in preparation.

Erich von Falkenhayn

French forces were taken by surprise when they were attacked on February 21. For nine hours, the Germans bombarded the area. The explosions were heard 150 miles away! As the bombs rained down, some French soldiers were buried alive by the flying dirt.

The Germans captured land and fortresses around Verdun. They cut the rail lines so the French could not use trains. This left the French with only a single, twenty-foot-wide gravel road to bring in troops and supplies.

This road was later named "the Sacred Way" because of its important role in keeping the French in the fight.

Hoping to divert the Germans' attention, the Allies launched the Battle of the Somme in July. For a week, British artillery bombed German defenses. But the German lines were too well prepared, sheltered from the bombing, and much of the German line remained intact. British soldiers charging across no-man's-land became easy targets.

After four months of fighting at the Somme, the Germans finally retreated. The British had recaptured just forty-eight square miles of land. The cost for this meager gain? One million killed or injured.

Meanwhile, nearly ten months after it began, the Battle of Verdun finally ended with a German retreat. More than seven hundred thousand people were killed or wounded on both sides,

70 percent by artillery fire. (By contrast, the Battle of Gettysburg—the US Civil War's deadliest—lasted just three days, with around fifty thousand casualties.)

Another of World War I's longest and deadliest battles took place at Gallipoli, in Turkey. The Ottoman Turks entered the war against Russia in October 1914 and began bombing Russian ports along the Black Sea and sinking ships. Right away,

the Allies wanted to help Russia knock Turkey out of the war.

In February 1915, Allied forces—including sixteen thousand troops from Australia and New Zealand—invaded Turkey. Turkish forces trapped them on a beach at Gallipoli. The Allies dug in, and a long, deadly stalemate ensued. Over eight months, more than one hundred thousand Turkish and Allied troops died. Swarms of flies, attracted to the beach by the bodies, spread disease throughout the trenches.

Don't Shoot the Messenger

In the days before cell phones, soldiers had to find creative ways to deliver urgent messages about battles. Enter the homing pigeon!

During World War I, more than half a million pigeons delivered messages rolled up into tiny canisters attached to the birds' legs. The pigeons lived in a coop at a command center. After they were taken away from the coop—to the battlefront, or dropped by parachute into enemy territory for spies to retrieve—the birds knew how to fly back to home base, carrying their "return" message!

One carrier pigeon, named Cher Ami (meaning "Dear Friend" in French), was awarded a medal of honor. He had delivered twelve important messages during his service. On his final trip, he was shot through the chest and leg. (He survived.)

Dogs also delivered message across battlefields. Some were even trained to lay down telegraph wire!

CHAPTER 4
Trench Warfare

With France to its west and Russia to its east, Germany would be fighting a war on two fronts. At the start of the war, German officials expected the massive Russian army would take at least six weeks to gather its troops. So Germany planned to invade France first. Their aim was to conquer Paris within forty-five days, before turning east to face Russia.

The Germans decided to invade France from the north, through Belgium. But Belgium was a neutral country. That means it had not taken sides.

Germany told Belgium: Allow us through, or be treated as an enemy. The Belgian king ignored Germany's threat. He had bridges, tunnels, and

railroad tracks destroyed to slow the Germans
down.

On August 4, 1914, the German army
invaded Belgium. They destroyed thousands of
buildings, torched entire villages, and murdered
or imprisoned thousands of civilians. But the
brave Belgian people kept the Germans out of
France for nearly a month. And Belgian soldiers
would continue to fight alongside Allied forces
for the remainder of the war.

The Battlefield Goes Global

World War I expanded quickly, in Europe and around the world. In 1915, Italy declared war on Austria-Hungary. The British fought the Ottoman Turks across their empire in the Middle East, from Egypt to Syria to Iraq to Arabia. Germany's African colonies were overtaken by French and British colonial troops. German ships battled the British Royal Navy off the Pacific and Atlantic coasts of South America. One German ship sank merchant, military, and passenger ships in the Indian Ocean, disrupting trade and spreading terror.

By 1918, twenty-seven nations had declared war against the Central Powers, though not every nation provided troops.

CENTRAL POWERS

Germany, Austria-Hungary,

Ottoman Empire, Bulgaria

ALLIED AND ASSOCIATED POWERS

Belgium, Bolivia, Brazil, the British Empire

(including Canada, Australia, New Zealand,

India, South Africa), China, Cuba, Czechoslovakia,

Ecuador, France, Greece, Guatemala, Haiti,

the Hejaz (Saudi Arabia), Honduras, Italy, Japan,

Liberia, Nicaragua, Panama, Peru, Poland,

Portugal, Romania, Serb-Croat-Slovene State,

Siam (Thailand), the United States, Uruguay

The Germans pushed to within thirty miles of Paris. Desperate to defend their capital, some six thousand Frenchmen rushed to the front, driven in six hundred Parisian taxicabs.

It turned out the Germans had advanced too quickly, and their supply lines couldn't keep up. Soldiers and horses were exhausted and hungry. They retreated fifty miles, then stationed themselves along a ridge, so they could see the Allies approaching. Then they dug trenches for protection.

But repeated Allied attacks were unable to

move the Germans from their position. So the Allies fell back and dug in, too.

Germany's plan had failed. There would be no swift victory in France. But neither were the Allies able to force Germany to surrender.

Over the next month, the armies raced north toward the English Channel, the narrow body of water separating Europe from Great Britain, each side trying to get around the other. They marched hundreds of miles, digging trenches along the way.

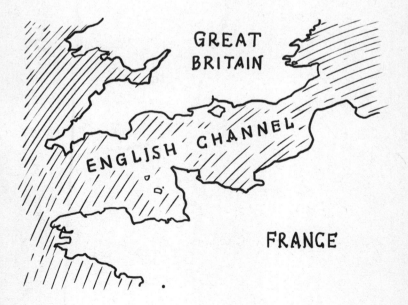

The Eastern Front

The Allies were able to prevent the Germans from invading Paris in part because Russia had rallied its troops faster than expected. Thousands of German soldiers had to leave the Western Front to face the Russian army along the thousand-mile-long Eastern Front.

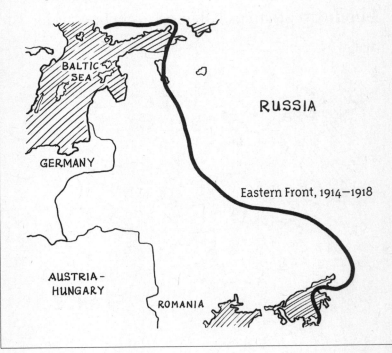

BALTIC SEA

RUSSIA

GERMANY

Eastern Front, 1914–1918

AUSTRIA-HUNGARY

ROMANIA

Russia's army was the largest in the world, but for the most part, troops were poorly equipped and badly trained. Germany had the strongest army. Germany also had an extensive system of roads and railways that helped transport troops and supplies quickly.

Russia invaded Germany on August 17, 1914. They were quickly pushed back. Farther south, Russia had better luck against the Austro-Hungarians. But Germany quickly came to their ally's aid and drove the Russians back east, capturing Russian territory along the way.

The Russian army was largely unsuccessful in its campaigns along the Eastern Front. However, because German troops were sent east, Russia had helped the Allies fighting in the west.

Soldiers lined the ditches with sandbags and barbed wire. They dug gun holes into the earthen walls, so they could shoot their guns without exposing themselves to enemy fire. They laid wooden boards called duckboards along the floors, to keep soldiers from sinking into the muddy ground.

Additional trenches were dug behind the front lines, where more troops were stationed. This

was in case the enemy overran the first line of trenches. Twisting, turning supply lines—easier to defend than straight pathways—reached back into the surrounding countryside. The lanes were sometimes named for well-known streets in the soldiers' home countries, so they wouldn't get lost.

Life in the trenches was miserable. The ditches were infested with rats and lice, which soldiers called "cooties." When it rained, the pathways became rivers of mud. "It was a . . . sucking kind of mud," said one soldier, ". . . a real monster that sucked at you." Nurse and poet Mary Borden called the muck of no-man's-land "the vast liquid grave of our armies."

Soldiers succumbed to illness easily in these conditions. "Trench foot" occurred when soldiers' feet remained cold and wet for too long. This led to pain, swelling, and infection. Sometimes the "trench foot" had to be amputated.

Thankfully, soldiers spent only a week to ten days at a time at the front lines. Then their days were spent in the reserve trenches or in the rear. There they received baths and clean clothing. While they were expected to drill, clean their kits, and attend lectures, they also rested. Far from the horrors of the trenches, soldiers relaxed in grassy fields, smoking cigarettes, reading, and writing  letters home. They played cards, formed sports clubs, played music, and even put on plays!

Back at the front lines, soldiers were regularly

called upon to charge out of the trenches and across no-man's-land. (The phrase "over the top" comes from these offensives.) Their goal was to dislodge the enemy and gain ground. In later years, tanks would join the charge.

Before the charge, heavy artillery fire weakened the enemy's defenses. "Now that I could hear these shells coming over," said one soldier, "I really began to know what fear was."

Because of the constant threat of attack—and the near-constant sound of bullets and bombs—soldiers in the trenches barely slept. Watch shifts were kept to two hours, because soldiers were so

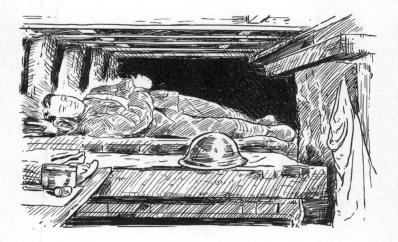

exhausted, they could barely keep their eyes open longer than that.

There were heavy casualties in trench warfare—and little to show for it. So on April 22, 1915, German troops used something new: poison gas. It was during an attack in Belgium, at Ypres (say: EE-pruh). The Germans opened six thousand cylinders of poison chlorine gas, at a time when the wind would carry it to the Allies. The greenish-yellow gas burned the soldiers' eyes and throats and filled their lungs with fluid.

The Allies quickly developed gas masks to protect their troops. Soldiers' horses also received gas masks. Over the course of the war, both sides invented new poison gases, like mustard gas.

In the end, approximately 1.2 million soldiers would be gassed. Many who survived were blistered or blinded for life. More than ninety thousand died.

CHAPTER 5
War in the Skies

When World War I began, aviation was still new. Orville and Wilbur Wright had flown the first motor-operated airplane just eleven years earlier. Planes were fragile—painted canvas stretched over

A British fighter airplane, the Sopwith Camel

a wood frame encasing the engine—and highly flammable. There were no navigational tools, and pilots became lost easily.

At first, planes were mainly "eyes in the sky." They flew over enemy lines to gather information about their position and weaponry. Pilots flew low to the ground, within range of antiaircraft guns. It was dangerous but crucial work.

If aviators encountered enemy aircraft, they might fire a pistol or throw a hand grenade at the other plane. Before long, planes were being outfitted with machine guns. Now aviators flew directly at each other in an aerial game of chicken, firing round after round of ammo.

Pilots flew upside down, in loops, and in circles to avoid being shot down. They attacked each other from behind and below. Eventually, a second, backward-facing seat was added to planes. From there, a "spotter" could see a plane approaching from the rear.

These dramatic midair battles were called dogfights. Once an aviator shot down five planes, he became an "ace." Aces were national heroes—celebrities, even—and their daring missions captured the public's imagination.

French ace René Fonck notched seventy-five hits. Britain's Albert Ball was just twenty years old by the time he downed forty-four planes, before being shot down and killed in 1917.

René Fonck

World War I's most successful ace was Baron Manfred von Richthofen—known as the "Red Baron" because of his scarlet-colored airplanes. He brought down eighty Allied aircraft. The Red Baron hired a German jeweler to engrave small silver cups with the date of each of his hits.

Manfred von Richthofen, the Red Baron

(That is, until German supplies of silver ran low.) He was killed in action on April 21, 1918.

In the early days of World War I, pilots would drop bombs by hand onto enemy lines. Soon, bomber planes were designed so a pilot could release his payload from the bottom of his aircraft with the flick of a switch.

The Germans were the first to bomb civilians. They did so from a terrifying new war machine: the zeppelin.

Developed by Count Ferdinand von Zeppelin in 1900, zeppelins were airships with a steel framework. They were filled with hydrogen gas, making them lighter than air. They flew higher than airplanes, and they were *huge*—more than six hundred feet long—and capable of carrying two tons of explosives.

After nightfall on January 19, 1915, two zeppelins crossed the English Channel. Witnesses said it was as if the airships had appeared out of nowhere, looking like floating cigars. Two English towns were bombed. Four people died.

The *Hindenburg*

After the war, zeppelins were used for luxury
air travel. Airships could cross the Atlantic Ocean in
under two days. Even the fastest ocean liners took
twice as long. But the era of airship travel was short-
lived, in part due to the fate of the *Hindenburg*.

At 804 feet long, the *Hindenburg*, built in 1936, was the largest airship ever. It featured a luxurious dining room and lounge, complete with a grand piano, and cabins for up to fifty passengers. Riders gazed out windows as the airship cruised through the skies.

On May 6, 1937, the *Hindenburg* was coming in for a landing at Lakehurst, New Jersey. At 7:25 p.m., a small flame rose from the tail section. In only thirty-four seconds, the entire ship was aflame. Passengers leaped from the *Hindenburg* as it crashed to the ground. Thirty-five of ninety-seven passengers and crew died.

On May 31, a zeppelin bombed London. Over the next year—on clear, moonless nights—the zeppelins returned more than fifty times. They rained fire down on the capital, killing hundreds.

The British set up better defenses in and around London. They installed giant searchlights.

They enforced curfews and blackouts at night, so airship pilots couldn't easily identify their targets. The pond in front of Buckingham Palace was drained, so it would not reflect light.

Soon, the British had airplanes that flew high enough to reach the zeppelins. The planes fired explosive bullets that pierced the airships' outer skin and ignited the hydrogen gas inside.

On September 2, 1916, during the biggest air raid on London, twenty-one-year-old William Leefe Robinson became the first British pilot to bring down a zeppelin. The explosion could be seen for one hundred miles around. Londoners cheered as the fiery airship fell to earth.

With the zeppelins' weakness exposed, the Germans turned to their two newest warplanes: the Gotha, a high-flying bomber, and the Riesenflugzeug ("Giant Aircraft"), with its 138-foot wingspan. British planes were no match for these massive aircraft.

Gotha

Britain was bombed mercilessly well into 1918, the war's final year. Hundreds of thousands of Londoners took shelter underground, sleeping in basements and subway stations.

The Germans thought their campaign of terror from the skies would break the British people's spirit and force their government to end the war. But they were wrong.

CHAPTER 6
War at Sea

For centuries, the British Royal Navy had dominated the world's oceans.

In 1906, the British unveiled the HMS *Dreadnought*, a battleship like no other. The *Dreadnought* traveled faster than any other ship at the time. It was the first battleship to mount only big, long-range guns—ten 12-inch guns,

HMS *Dreadnought*

twenty-four 3-inch quick-firing guns, five machine guns, and five torpedo tubes.

The *Dreadnought* ushered in a frantic period of shipbuilding. *Dreadnought*-style ships got bigger and bigger—so big, in fact, that the *Dreadnought* soon became outdated. A new class of "super-dreadnought" ships became the norm.

Germany had also been building up its navy. Still, by the start of the war, the Royal Navy's fleet significantly outnumbered the German High Seas Fleet. But neither side wanted a direct conflict—particularly Germany. For the British, protecting their merchant ships around the world was more important than destroying German ships.

Rather than attack Germany, the British wanted to cut it off from the world. So they imposed a blockade to prevent food, fuel, and supplies from reaching the country. Ships could not sail to or from Germany without being stopped by the

Royal Navy. The blockade also kept the German navy trapped at home and unable to assist German troops on the global battlefield.

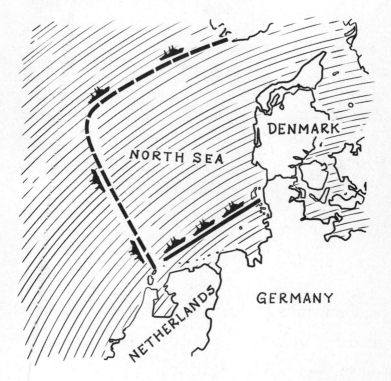

In response, the Germans deployed the U-boat.

Unterseeboot (say: OON-tehr-see-boot) means "undersea boat" in German. These submarines were more than two hundred feet long and carried thirty-five men and twelve torpedoes. Like the airplane, the submarine was relatively new.

U-Boat

Germany's U-boats were the most advanced in the world. They cruised unseen beneath the waves, right past the British blockade. (Sonar technology to detect objects underwater was not invented until after the war.)

The British dropped huge nets to try to trap the U-boats. They set off underwater bombs.

They even tried to camouflage the hulls of their ships by painting them to look like the water's surface, thinking this would make them harder to spot from below. (It did not work.)

Germany decided to impose a blockade of their own on the British. They declared the waters surrounding Great Britain to be a war zone. Any ship delivering supplies there—even a ship from a neutral country like the United States—could be destroyed.

The German U-boats sank many ships, but supplies still reached Great Britain. Meanwhile, the British blockade of Germany was holding strong. Hundreds of German citizens were dying of starvation every day. The German navy had to win control over the North Sea.

The Battle of Jutland (May 31–June 1, 1916) was the largest naval battle of World War I. It took place off the coast of Denmark's Jutland Peninsula. Two hundred fifty ships and one hundred thousand men took part.

Britain's HMS *Indefatigable* and HMS *Queen Mary* both exploded when German shells hit their ammunition stores. Admiral Sir David Beatty directed his battle cruisers to pull back and wait for reinforcements from Admiral of the Fleet John Jellicoe. Once Jellicoe's fleet arrived, the German High Seas Fleet was outnumbered and returned home.

The British lost more than six thousand sailors and fourteen ships. The Germans lost fewer men and ships, but they did not win the battle. The British blockade remained.

American Neutrality

Most Americans did not want to get involved in World War I. In 1914, US president Woodrow Wilson declared America's neutrality. The United States would not pick sides. Wilson won reelection in 1916, in part because of one of his campaign slogans: "He kept us out of war."

Woodrow Wilson

Still, many in the United States viewed Germany as the aggressor—the country that started the war. So the United States provided the Allies with lots of money, weapons, and supplies to fight the Central Powers. Some Americans even went overseas to join Allied armies.

CHAPTER 7
The United States Enters the War

At first, before sinking a merchant ship, German U-Boat commanders offered crews a chance to escape. This was because merchant ships were not involved in battle. Some British warships, however, were disguised as ordinary ships. And soon, Germany was torpedoing ships without warning—even passenger ships.

When it was built in 1906, the 787-foot-long RMS *Lusitania* was the largest—and fastest—

RMS *Lusitania*

ocean liner in the world. With room on board for nearly 2,200 passengers, the *Lusitania* featured electric lights and elevators!

For years, the *Lusitania* ferried passengers between Liverpool, England, and New York City. Crossing the ocean was like taking a luxury vacation. But on May 7, 1915, a German U-boat torpedoed the ship off the coast of Ireland.

The *Lusitania* sank in less than twenty minutes. Nearly 1,200 people died, including 128 Americans.

Public opinion in America turned sharply against Germany. President Wilson demanded an end to Germany's attacks. Germany agreed to stop sinking ships without giving warning, and to not attack passenger ships.

But Germans were suffering under the British blockade. Desperate to impose similar pain on Britain, Germany eventually broke its promise and once again began sinking ships without warning. In just three months, U-boats sank another five hundred merchant ships. (Over the course of the war, they would sink more than five thousand.)

Germany knew their actions risked bringing the United States into the war. But in the end, it was a telegram that did the trick.

On February 24, 1917, British spies delivered a shocking message to President Wilson. Germany had sent a secret telegram to Mexico. A German official named Arthur Zimmermann was proposing a German–Mexican alliance if the United States entered the war. He even offered to help Mexico invade the United States if that happened!

Arthur Zimmermann

When newspapers reported on the Zimmermann telegram, public support to join the war grew.

On April 2, Wilson asked the US Congress for a declaration of war on Germany. (According to the US Constitution, only Congress can do that.) "The world must be made safe for democracy," Wilson said. Four days later, the United States was at war.

Americans got to work immediately. Production of weapons and supplies soared. Posters and other advertising campaigns encouraged everyone to do their part by joining the military or purchasing war bonds to raise money. Families planted "victory gardens" in their backyards, so more food could be sent overseas.

In 1914, the US army was only the seventeenth-largest in the world, smaller than Serbia's. On the day the United States joined the war, there were just over 125,000 in the army. Many volunteered to serve, but it would not be enough.

Local draft boards were established to call men ages twenty-one to thirty-one into service. This was not a choice. By the war's end, four million American men—seven out of ten of whom were drafted—had served in the armed forces.

Recruits were sent to training camps across the country. Many of these Americans were children of immigrants from the very countries at war in Europe. When it came time to ship off, most departed from New York City, under the gaze of the Statue of Liberty.

After three years of war, French and British troops needed help badly. They were exhausted. Many had died. Thousands of French troops had mutinied, refusing to fight anymore.

The war had also grown unpopular among Russians. In December 1917, Russia signed an

armistice, or a formal agreement to end military operations, with the Central Powers. With the battle on the Eastern Front over, the Germans turned back westward.

The United States had joined the war not a moment too soon. But would it be too late?

Revolution in Russia

Tsar Nicholas II had no military experience, and he mismanaged the war effort. Factories couldn't produce weapons quickly enough. This left troops to fight empty-handed or lift weapons from the bodies of their fallen comrades. Millions had died, been captured, or been injured.

In February 1917, food shortages and rising prices led to revolution. Soldiers joined their fellow citizens on strike, calling for an end to Nicholas II's reign. In March, the tsar's advisers convinced him to step down, ending three centuries of Nicholas's family's rule. (The next year, Nicholas II and his family were killed by the revolutionaries.)

A temporary government was set up, but in November a revolution brought Vladimir Lenin and the Communists to power. Lenin signed a

Vladimir Lenin

treaty with the Central Powers, ending Russian involvement in the war.

In 1922, the Union of Soviet Socialist Republics (USSR) was formed. The Soviet Union lasted until the end of 1991, when it was dissolved into fifteen independent countries, the largest being Russia, Kazakhstan, and Ukraine.

CHAPTER 8
Women in the War

Women played a major role in World War I. As millions of men were called to military service, women stepped in to take their jobs. From factories to farms to police forces, women were going to work!

American women also served on the front lines. Twenty thousand joined the Army Nurse Corps, which had been founded in 1901; it was the first time women had served officially in the US military. They drove trucks and ambulances; worked as mechanics, electricians, and telephone operators; and more. Millions more volunteered for the Red Cross and other organizations that provided aid.

In Great Britain, women served in the Royal

Air Force and the Royal Navy. More than one hundred thousand joined the Women's Land Army, which helped the war effort through farming.

Women from Russia, Bulgaria, Romania, and Serbia fought on the front lines. The Russian Women's Battalion of Death was noted for its bravery in battle.

In France, the scientist Marie Curie—the first woman to win a Nobel Prize—wanted to find her own way of helping. Marie had discovered the element radium. Radium was used in X-rays.

At the time, X-ray machines were available only in city hospitals. Now they were needed in battle to help wounded soldiers. So Marie Curie invented a small car containing X-ray equipment that could be driven to the battlefield. She raised money from wealthy Parisians and built twenty of these "little Curies." She trained 150 women to operate them. More than one million X-rays were taken because of Marie Curie's work, saving many lives.

Marie Curie

Women everywhere answered the call to serve, despite not having the same rights as men at home. In the United States, women had been working—for years—to win the right to vote.

President Wilson had never supported women's suffrage. But after seeing how American women had helped the war effort, he changed his views.

In 1918, Wilson made his case in a speech to the US Senate. He said, "This war could not have been fought . . . if it had not been for the services of the women."

Two years later, the Nineteenth Amendment to the Constitution was ratified. At last, American women could vote. By defending democracy overseas, women had secured their own rights at home. Though it is important to note that unfair laws in Southern states continued to bar many Black people from voting until the mid-1960s.

CHAPTER 9
Here Come the Doughboys!

By March 1918, more than three hundred thousand American soldiers—popularly called "Doughboys"—had arrived in France, with more arriving daily. (By the end of the war, two million would serve overseas.)

The American Expeditionary Forces (AEF), which included US Marines, were under the command of General John Joseph "Black Jack" Pershing. General Pershing began training his troops while British and French soldiers held the line against the Germans.

German general Erich Ludendorff saw a final opportunity to defeat the Allies. Rather than bombard the enemy with explosives for days, the Germans launched fast surprise attacks against unprepared Allied troops.

General John Joseph Pershing

The Germans advanced forty miles into Allied territory, toward Paris. On April 2, Pershing agreed to send American troops to the front line.

The fresh and battle-ready Doughboys helped push the Germans back.

On June 6, US Marines fought at Belleau Wood, east of Paris. It was the deadliest day in the Marines' history up to that point, with 222 killed. Although advised to retreat, they continued fighting for nearly three weeks before finally retaking the woods. Legend says that German soldiers called them "Teufelshunde," meaning "Devil Dogs"—a nickname that sticks to this day.

The Germans kept attacking into the summer but failed to gain ground. From mid-July onward, the Allies and the Doughboys had them on the run.

On September 26, one of the war's final battles began in northwestern France. More than six hundred thousand French and American troops—and five hundred tanks and airplanes—advanced on German forces along the Meuse River and into the Argonne Forest.

The Harlem Hellfighters

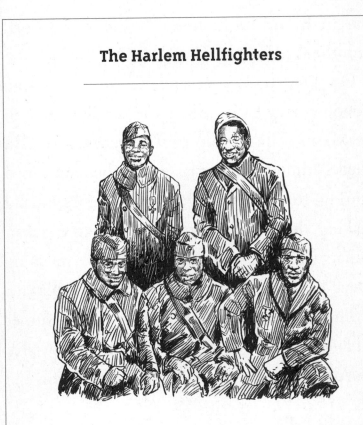

The 369th Infantry Regiment also earned a fearsome nickname from German soldiers: "Hollenkampfer," or "Hellfighters." The regiment's soldiers were mostly from Harlem, a Black neighborhood in New York City.

Black Americans did not have equal rights in

their own country. So why should they go to battle to defend European democracy, many asked. Lynchings—public executions of Black people by white mobs without judge and jury—were occurring weekly. President Wilson himself screened a racist film at the White House. It glorified the Ku Klux Klan, a white terrorist group that lynched many Black Americans.

Still, many Black men enlisted. But America's armed forces were segregated—Black soldiers could not serve alongside white soldiers. And most Black soldiers were assigned menial tasks.

French troops were not segregated. So the Harlem Hellfighters fought with the French! They spent more than six months in combat, longer than any other American unit. France awarded the Hellfighters medals for their bravery.

The Battle of Meuse-Argonne raged for nearly seven weeks. More than twenty-six thousand Americans died. To this day, it remains the deadliest battle in US history. But finally, the

Germans were nearly pushed out of France. By October 5, they were overrun along the entire Western Front.

Meanwhile, the Austro-Hungarian Empire was coming apart at the seams. Nations within its borders had begun declaring their independence. Hungary and Austria's dual monarchy had imploded. On November 3, the empire agreed to a cease-fire with Italy.

On November 7, German officials met with the Allied commander-in-chief in Compiègne, France, to discuss a cease-fire. Kaiser Wilhelm II was forced to abdicate the throne and flee Germany. On November 11, 1918, an armistice was signed, ending the fighting.

The news reached New York City at three in the morning. People awoke to wailing sirens and cheering neighbors everywhere. Businesses all around the city closed for the day. Soldiers who had already returned home were cheered, hugged, and kissed by revelers. The celebration continued all day and night.

Jubilant scenes like this played out across the globe. "This tragical war," President Wilson said to Congress later that day, "whose consuming flames swept from one nation to another, until all the world was on fire, is at an end."

Veterans Day

The day World War I ended, President Wilson wrote, "Armistice Day will be filled with solemn pride in the heroism of those who died in the country's service." In the coming years, states began declaring Armistice Day an official holiday. It became a national holiday in 1938. After World War II, November 11 became a holiday to honor veterans of all wars: Veterans Day.

CHAPTER 10
The Treaty of Versailles

To be sure, the end of the war was cause for joy. However, would there be a lasting peace? Woodrow Wilson had ideas for making this happen. In fact, he had fourteen! In a 1918 speech, President Wilson outlined what he called the Fourteen Points, a plan for the world to follow to achieve peace and security.

The first point called for an end to secret treaties between nations. Another point called for reducing weapons of war. Most central to Wilson's

Fourteen Points was the League of Nations.

The League of Nations would be a group of countries working together to resolve disputes before they broke out into war. Also, if one member in the League was attacked, other members would come to its defense.

Peace talks began in Paris on January 18, 1919. Delegates from almost thirty countries attended, but the "Big Four" were in charge—

Vittorio Orlando, David Lloyd George,
Georges Clemenceau, and Woodrow Wilson

President Wilson, Prime Minister David Lloyd George of Great Britain, Prime Minister Vittorio Orlando of Italy, and Prime Minister Georges Clemenceau of France. (The defeated powers were not invited; Russia did not attend.) The Big Four agreed on one major point: Germany must be made so weak, it could never wage war again.

The final agreement was signed at the Palace of Versailles (say: vehr-SIGH) on June 28, 1919—exactly five years after the assassination of Archduke Franz Ferdinand. The terms of the Treaty of Versailles were severe.

Palace of Versailles

The German army was cut from nearly two million troops to one hundred thousand. The navy was greatly reduced; there could be no more U-boats. Germany was forbidden to have an air force. Ten percent of German land in Europe went to other countries, including the newly independent nation of Poland. Germany also lost all its overseas territories.

Finally, Germany was forced to accept full responsibility for the war, including paying for all the damage caused. (This is called reparations.) That amount in US money today would be half a *trillion* dollars.

With the stroke of a pen, Germany's economy was blown to pieces. Soon, Germans' paper money would be worthless. They needed wheelbarrows to carry home their weekly wages.

Is it any wonder peace couldn't last even twenty years?

CHAPTER 11
Legacy

A war's end doesn't bring back the dead or heal the wounded. Few European families escaped the devastation of World War I, whether they lost a son to enemy fire, a grandmother to disease or starvation, or their hometown to an invading army. Many surviving soldiers experienced shell shock, trauma caused by the horrors of war. (Today, shell shock is known as post-traumatic stress disorder, or PTSD.)

The Treaty of Versailles led to the creation of the League

of Nations, but the US Senate voted not to join. Lawmakers worried about getting drawn into another war in Europe.

President Wilson tried to sell the idea to the American people. He traveled eight thousand miles around the country in less than a month. Wilson suffered a stroke on the trip that nearly killed him. The United States never became a member of the League of Nations.

Still, by the end of 1920, forty-eight countries had joined the league. For the next twenty years,

League of Nations

the league settled several minor disputes. But in other cases, it was ineffective.

In the 1930s, many Germans turned to a new leader, Adolf Hitler. He blamed Germany's problems on minority populations, including Jews, the Roma, and queer people. He promised a return to greatness for the German people. Defying the terms

Adolf Hitler

of the Treaty of Versailles, he began building up Germany's military.

In 1939, Hitler invaded Poland, and Great Britain and France declared war on Germany. Peace in Europe had not held. History was already repeating itself. And there was little doubt what to call this latest global catastrophe: the Second World War.

Flanders Fields

There is an area in Belgium called Flanders Fields, where a million soldiers died during the war. Before the war, beautiful red poppies had grown there. Soldiers sometimes pressed poppies into their letters home.

John McCrae was a Canadian soldier and surgeon who treated the wounded. He wrote a famous poem called "In Flanders Fields" after the death of a close friend. The poem reads in part:

> In Flanders fields the poppies blow
> Between the crosses, row on row,
> That mark our place; and in the sky
> The larks, still bravely singing, fly
> Scarce heard amid the guns below.

We are the Dead. Short days ago
We lived, felt dawn, saw sunset glow,
Loved and were loved, and now we lie,
In Flanders fields.

Because of McCrae's poem, the poppy became a symbol of the ultimate sacrifice borne by fallen soldiers. Wearing a poppy became a way to honor those who died for their country. Today, almost twelve thousand soldiers are buried at Tyne Cot, a cemetery in West Flanders. Most of them are identified only as "A Soldier of the Great War, Known Unto God."

Timeline of World War I

1914 — June 28: Archduke Franz Ferdinand of Austria-Hungary assassinated by a Serbian nationalist

July 28: Austria-Hungary declares war on Serbia

Aug. 4: Germany invades Belgium; US president Woodrow Wilson declares American neutrality

Aug. 17: Russia invades Germany on the Eastern Front

Sept. 6–12: Allies save Paris at First Battle of the Marne

1915 — Jan. 19: First zeppelin attack on British soil

Apr. 22: Germans use poison gas against Allies at Ypres, Belgium

May 7: German U-boat sinks the RMS *Lusitania* off the coast of Ireland

1916 — Feb. 21–Dec. 18: Battle of Verdun, World War I's longest

1917 — Feb. 24: Zimmermann telegram between Germany and Mexico shown to President Wilson

Apr. 6: United States declares war on Germany

Dec. 15: Russia and Central Powers sign an armistice

1918 — Sept. 26–Nov. 11: Battle of Meuse-Argonne, deadliest in US history

Nov. 11: Germany signs an armistice

1919 — Peace talks begin in Paris in January

June 28: Treaty of Versailles signed

Timeline of the World

1914 — Jan. 1: World's first commercial flight, from St. Petersburg to Tampa, Florida

— Feb. 7: Debut of Charlie Chaplin's character the Tramp

— Aug. 15: Panama Canal opens

— Sept. 1: World's last living passenger pigeon, named Martha, dies at the Cincinnati Zoo

1915 — Jan. 25: Transcontinental phone service opens between San Francisco and New York

— Apr. 7: Jazz singer Billie Holiday born in Philadelphia

— May 6: Babe Ruth hits first major league home run

1916 — Apr. 12: Children's author Beverly Cleary born in McMinnville, Oregon

— Apr. 24–29: In Easter Rising, Irish republicans unsuccessfully rebel against British rule

— July 1–12: Four deadly shark attacks occur in New Jersey

— Sept. 11: First supermarket opens, the Piggly Wiggly in Memphis, Tennessee

1917 — Apr. 3: Georgia O'Keeffe's first one-woman art show

— June 8: Walt Disney graduates from high school

1918 — Influenza epidemic begins, killing as many as one hundred million people worldwide by 1920

Bibliography

*Books for young readers

*Adams, Simon. *Eyewitness: World War I*. New York: DK
Publishing, 2014.

History.com Editors. "World War I." *A&E Television Networks*,
2009. https://www.history.com/topics/world-war-i/world-
war-i-history.

Ives, Stephen, Amanda Pollak, and Rob Rapley, dirs. *American
Experience: The Great War: A Nation Comes
of Age*. Insignia Films, 2017.

Keegan, John. *The First World War*. New York: Vintage Books,
2000.

Levy, Daniel S. *LIFE: World War I: The Great War and the
American Century*. New York: Time Inc. Books, 2017.

Steele, Ben, director. *The First World War*. Arrow Films, 2003.

Tuchman, Barbara W. *The Guns of August: The Outbreak of World War I*. New York: Random House Trade Paperbacks, 2014.

*Turner, Daniel. *A Simple Guide to World War I: Centenary Edition*. London: Simple History, 2014.

Websites

Library of Congress: Echoes of the Great War: American Experiences of World War I

https://www.loc.gov/exhibitions/world-war-i-american-experiences/about-this-exhibition/

The United States World War One Centennial Commission: Articles and Topics

https://www.worldwar1centennial.org/index.php/edu-home/edu-topics.html

Archduke Franz Ferdinand and Sophie minutes before their assassination

British soldiers line up in a trench in 1914.

A crowd of new recruits for the US army in 1918

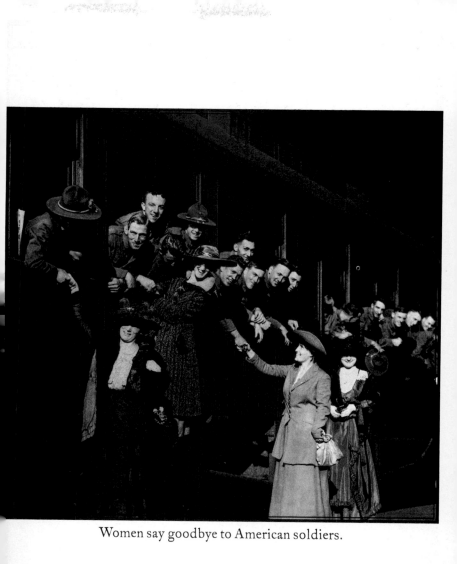
Women say goodbye to American soldiers.

American troops use French tanks.

Dogs pull a machine gun used by the Belgian army.

Marie Curie drives a "little Curie" car with X-ray equipment in 1914.

British tanks move toward the front lines.

21

A priest with soldiers in a makeshift hospital in Russia

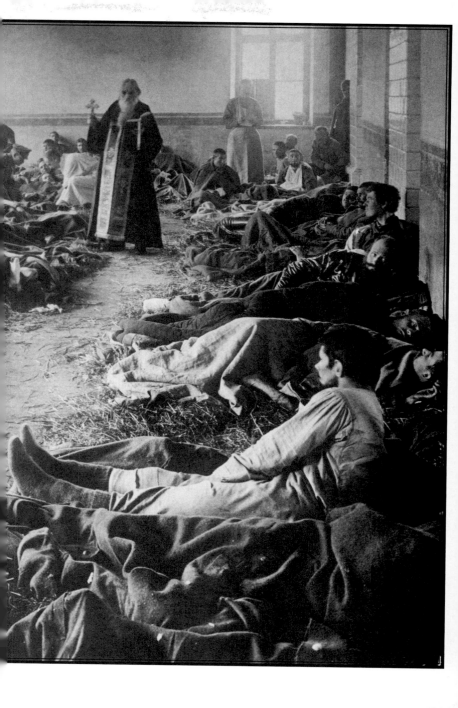

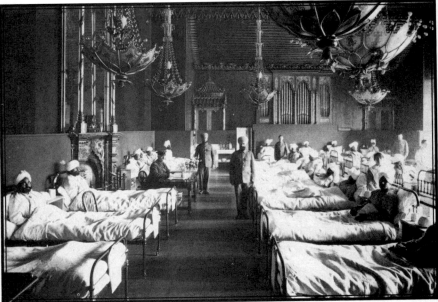

Wounded Indian soldiers of the British army at the Brighton Pavilion in 1915

French troops walk through ruins in Verdun, France.

The wreckage after battle in Ypres, Belgium

Tanzanian troops under German command

Australian troops set up camp near the Pyramids in Egypt.

In the Alps, Italian troops on skis advance on Austrian forces.

A dog jumps over barbed wire in Belgium to deliver a message.

British civilians with a surrendered German U-boat

A parade in New York City honors the return of the Black troops of the 369th Infantry.

The signing of the Treaty of Versailles in the Hall of Mirrors